# Hot air



Asher Haynes

BookLeaf Publishing

Presentation by *BookLeaf Publishing*

Web: www.bookleafpub.com

E-mail: info@bookleafpub.com

ISBN: 9789357446198

First edition 2023

*To Babba*

# ACKNOWLEDGEMENT

Mr P, for helping me to realise my words could be heard and appreciated.

# I am not a debate

Despite what They say,
i didn't decide
to turn out this way.

And now They divide
The 'us' and The 'Them'.
With bills to abide

to mask up the fem
They want to abate,
As They try to bend

'em back into shape:
When did life
become a debate?

# on the man who saw her tiny coffin in the back of the hearse

he took of his cap
and lowered his head-

'dear God, it's a baby'
his wife had said.

# Medicated pt.1

I picked up my first prescription
At a pharmacy a few towns over-
As was my custom
Before I realised people wouldn't
Talk about me and my meds.

Signed for the
'Controlled substance'
that gives me control.

Over my brain
And my life
No more feigning
The realisation
Of normality.

I placed the innocuous blue and white
Pill on my tongue
Took a swig
Swilled it back

It's in. Is it working?
No you fool, it's been 2 seconds
When does it start working?
I don't know, give it time.

The dialogue hadn't stopped yet.
I sent a quick prayer
to the unknown pharmacology god
For the chatter to cease .

And soon, it had.
The world was quiet
I worked through the thoughts
That didn't argue anymore

My pills are red and white now
My dose went up
I take extra ones too.

The new ones aren't as colourful
But they make my life
Less monochrome

They 'take the edge off'
As my mom says
They take me off the edge

Of something bigger

# Medicated pt.2

At a talk about sleep,
He asked: ‘how does your energy shift?’
Everyone’s graphs looked the same:
An optimistic upward slope-
D
R
O
P
Followed by that post-dinner burst.
Mine didn’t look like that.

‘Idunnominearebasedonwhenitakemymeds’
Which were evidently wearing off
No ‘normal’ person talks that quickly.
The eye contact was awkward
To say the least-
Quasi-sympathetic interrogations,
Pupil to pupil.

0600 4 pills-
1600 2 pills-
2100 2 pills (or 3 if it has been a rough day)-
Head up for tablets,
Head down for capsules.
A settled routine
To help me keep mine.

But an existence
Reliant on chemicals
Just isn’t the same

As living like
Everyone else
Who get through on

Carbohydrates, proteins
And the occasional
Simple sugar.

Receptors lit up against their will,
Though they ache and beg,
The midnight main-beam
Scours B roads
Until the next street lights.

# An artist unknown

He had never spent so long
in the studio until
That Winter-doused
in frost and a burning desire
to thaw his ridiculed asceticism.

Mocked in Cyprus, he
fled, seeking a safehouse
among real men and girls.
To reside where tradition
would allow him to

deride those egotists
who dared to call his
Chivalry 'Chauvinist'-
What hokum to claim of
A man of such assured grace.

And so he set to work:
wedging, rolling
pulling and moulding.
Throughout the darker months,
he raised her from batt

to rafter. Fettled her edges.
She was hollow, of course
He'd never bear the extra weight,
but he added coiling
where he felt it necessary.

Though liberal with bentonite,
he knew she'd never move-
as was ideal-all he needed was
a little flex and pressure.
Too much and she'd know her worth

outside of his craft.
Maybe she'd even think he cared. No,
it was for the best.
If she could speak back, she'd
just be a woman.

Still, he recited her purpose
like a mantra as he glazed.
And prayed Aphrodite would not
mistake him for another
lonely, soulless sculptor.

He was an Artist, not some
potter wanting more, so if
art is to be enjoyed,
why shouldn't he fulfill his role?
Servant of Hephaestus

(And Eros, some say)
But he pushed too far-
as all men do.
The delicate ceramic
cracked and splintered-

Shattered like starlight-
the the kind that sent the
less-educated squealing
to temple steps.
He was back to wedging.

# fast fashion makes for a slow death

‘Retro Vintage Nostalgic
Denim-style Unique
Fashion Jeans’

A wolf in sweatshop clothing-
shouldn’t be exposed
to a naked flame

or the whole factory goes up.
With the gates locked
to ‘prevent stealing’.

But who is the real thief
when the buckling limbs
that reach through

the bars,
are the same ones
they tried to cover
with thin polyester.
Because they’re paid in pennies
and not enough change?

Still, they work as fast
as fashion wants them to.

# The lapse I keep from her

I walked this path, with her far behind
Found it surrendered like the distant west;
Laid my hand on her shoulder, and it to rest-
in closer quarters, she will never find.

# Rat trap

'Try eating my cables now you little shit'

A quick trip to B&Q was all it took.
He was practically drooling as he payed.
The cashier, a plucky 16 year old
with a pink strip in her hair

lost a little of her sparkle
when she saw his excitement.
'How about something more…
humane?'

Humane? What did she take him for?
Woke nonsense!
He needed the thrill-
to feel Death in his bones.
he'd hang, draw and quarter it
if the little bugger weren't so quick.

Carlsberg in hand, he set the traps-
Eight in total (he was not letting that thing
escape).

Like a tiger suspended on its hind legs,
Poised to pounce-

he slumped on the recliner in the living room.
it exhaled a gulp of stale tobacco smoke
As he waited, impatiently, for his catch.

It was done.
Almost.
The brute stumbled up the stairs towards
the keening symbol of man's true power.

He was the grim reaper.
His robe: a Homer Simpson dressing gown
from 12 Christmases ago.
His scythe: a sterling superking.

He pined in the aftermath.
Not for the rat,
for the thrill
for something to do
to fill his days outside of Jeremy Kyle
And builders' brews.
He'd never been one for picking on someone his
own size.

# Red 2+Yellow 5

He'd been feeling a little blue,
so put saccharine in his tea.
He'd never added sugar
but was seeking something sweet.

He chose the 'healthy' option
for fear of rotten teeth.
But he only found it sickly,
as if a marching fleet

of Wellness Girls with their
Chunky-Knit White Jumpers,
had descended around him
to drag him out his slump

kicking and screaming…
He spat out the tea, dumped
it down the drain.
He let the blue back in-

smoothed over every inch of brain.
He didn't force an orange filter
of 'Golden Hour' dreams,
he knew better

than to cover the blue
or try and intervene.
So he sat with his tea,
and quietly asked me

To ‘Never buy saccharine’.

# Guerlain Samsara Eau de Parfum

Windows vista
and Fireman Sam.
The dial-up tone
and comfort by the kilogram.

Apricot yoghurt
and felt-tip pens.
The old collie, George,
when joy would never end.

A baby 'blanket',
yet I was flanked with
a zebra-print scarf,
that smelled like
cigarette smoke
and Samsara.

Until they discontinued it.

# Tie-Dye

The old man,
who lives down the road,
wears his soul
on his jacket sleeve-
over his shirt,
colour coordinated of course.
With a pocket
to hold his pipe in a pouch.

I know my Dad
by his rock-band t-shirts
and shorts, even
if the snow reaches the hem-
a solid routine.
Though, some of his shirts
he gave to me,
swamped: from shoulder to knee.

My Mom is
The Queen of Cozy Jumpers
fine-knit things-
and still, she complains about
'another wool load'.
With her soft leather boots-
fur-lined
to keep her ankles warm.

I suppose that’s why my clothes
are eclectic-
If we are what we wear.
The arrays of
colours and patterns, too
hard to match
strewn across the carpet, and
I’m okay with that.

# Omega 3

For workplace stress,
we take every herbal remedy.
Fill in every workbook
for ‘low mood’ and anxiety

in neat handwriting-
like a suicide note in cursive.
When all that’s left for me,
is a coat-hanger lobotomy.

# Stardust

My body is made of stardust:
Each breath, every heartbeat.
Does that mean I must

be some kind of elite?
An alien space ranger,
from a Martian space fleet.

Or is it more strange
that you're stardust too?
Intergalactic interchange

sent you here to do
The Earthly Tasks
expected of you.

Would it be wrong to ask
you not to hate the
'Stardust outcast'

Or do you not see
The paths of the
Stardust family tree?

# Connected

Electronic headphones
to block out urban noise-
to hide from the unknowns
of her robotic voice.

I listen to the birds
once or twice a week:
when I'm using one earbud,
incase someone chases me,
On my early morning run.

# The Fiery Fields

They'd always been called that
but I'd never known why.
Turns out it was
far more self-explanatory
than I had thought:

So now I sit in the soot-
stained, hollow stumps
while the dog stalks through the bushes.
and conjure a memory
That isn't mine

of the pits gently smouldering
from a fire that had been smothered
after the frantic shouts of
families and farmers.
How long had the flames
Licked up through the ground,
Rinsed this trunk from the inside out?
Did they try and fight it from their level,
Or did they know the damage
Had to be done
To be salvaged in the future?
Not that it has been.
The grass is tenacious, of course

but the logs are still hollow.
They'll rot one day and then,
I suppose,
a new tree grows

# A Cup of Tea and a Bath

They say a cup of tea can fix anything, so

I'd dragged my bones
to the kitchen
Heaved my feet down
each step as
Steep as the last.

And as I waited for
The click, was thinking:
How proud I was
That I'd made is this far.

I unscrewed the cap
of the carton
-because I don't drink enough
to keep it in fresh

Then watched as
my arm wouldn't
tilt back-and I was left
with an absolute mess

A tea too milky
Could my day get worse?

I’d say I tipped it out
And made another,
But to be honest
I couldn’t be bothered.

# My Love Was Blind

I miss the disco lights
In the living room:
Because, you see
That was all she could see
Not that it ever bothered me-

I miss the long nights
Under the rainbow moon,
Of cuddles with her
Nothing else she'd prefer
Than sinking into a golden slumber

I want to pinch her cheeks
Count her little fingers
and toes, in rows of five,
To just stay inside
With that baby, so full of joy, and life

I want back the weeks
I haven't been with her,
Too long are the nights
Without her art my side
Smiling, under the disco lights.

# Wisdom

She imparts her wisdom
Like her offer of biscuits
Daily, only to be
a wee bit upset
When I don't accept

always there
When the craic isn't 90
With her dad jokes
And her hobnobs-
Even though I don't like biscuits

# Lavender

After the shining sunflowers
We seek the subtle, gentle-
After rumination hours
When I need an ear

for my ramblings.
I find it at her desk,
When my mind is in shambles
She's there to say:

'I've got you' and
'You will be okay'

www.ingramcontent.com/pod-product-compliance
Lightning Source LLC
Chambersburg PA
CBHW051752130826
49812CB00033B/1109
*9789357446198*